Imaginary Friends:
Not Just Kid Stuff

Ravyn Karasu

Copyright © 2016 Ravyn Karasu

All rights reserved.

Special Thanks

I really wanted to give a lot of thanks to my professors, to my friends, my family, and to those that have volunteered their time to make this research possible.

ABSTRACT

The idea of imaginary friends (creative companions) is pretty standard in the realm of child psychology. However, we never really see anything substantial about the notion of these companions in adolescents and adults, let alone the purpose or effects of those companions on those individuals. Adolescents and adults tend to face more negative stigmas than that of children, yet also use their companions in a way that is more complex yet similarly to developing children. According to both the literature and personal study, older individuals aren't just developing important skills, but also maintaining creative thinking on multiple levels in regards to several areas of mental and social skills. The personal study involved employed a set of interview questions for volunteers to answer and discuss involving their current creative companions. As such, the study was to investigate if creative companions were present in teens and adults without a major negative psychosis and are they common. If so, what were the stigmas as well as the benefits? The study was favorable and in agreement with the information available in literary studies, as well as showing a set of patterns and functionality in the creators of companions. While stigmas were present, volunteers showed favorable preference to creating and maintaining companions, not to reject social interaction, but to enhance it as well as develop creative skills, self-therapy, and personal entertainment for the self and others. The results then open the door to realizing how potentially common the practice is, the positive utilization and experience of creative companions, and the unfair stigma of what these companionships have in our society.

INTRODUCTION

Me & My Shadows

I live in a world full of imagination. One could even say that people like me are like gods, with our ability to both create and destroy to our hearts' content. What do I mean by that? The concept of blasphemy isn't at work in this case. I am a writer. My specialty is fiction stories. My entire existence in the writing field depends on the ability to create, utilize, and form relationships with characters that do not exist in our reality. The thing is, I've done this my entire life.

As a child, I used to play a *lot* of pretend. I was one of those kids that had few friends, but the importance was in the quality, not the quantity.

Whether or not I was in the presence of these childhood playmates didn't matter. When we were together, we'd create stories with characters we enjoyed in our favorite movies, shows, and storybooks. Sometimes we'd make up some new ones. When I was alone, I'd create characters, again, either as a group of original characters, established fan favorites, or a mix of both to go on imaginary adventures. I didn't have imaginary friends as in a single entity or multiple entities with a solid existence. My imaginary companions had a purpose in keeping me entertained and/or to fuel an interest in something through influence. The point is that, while I didn't have the stereotypical imaginary friend, I still had imaginary companions. Not only did I have those companions, but I continued to have those types of companions as I grew up. To this day, I still have some. Sometimes they change, sometimes, they rotate. Sometimes, they are established characters, sometimes they are entirely new ones or modified ones.

Growing up, I continued to keep few friends and even developed trust issues. I was lonely and bored, so creating characters to entertain me became the norm. I was able to explore the many alternate universes of worlds I enjoyed. I even indulged in writing fanfiction. I also would write original works, and I would daydream endlessly about anything and everything. The world of imagination was like the endless world of Fantasia in *The Neverending Story*. There were just no limits.

That may be well and good, but what does this have to do with imaginary friends? I've never had the stereotypical sort. I didn't have any *Nadines* or *Drop Dead Freds* or *Harveys*. What I had were the silent companions, for the most part. Not only were they not seen by others, but they were virtually non-existent in the "real world." You'd never know that my silent days were spent on grand adventures, pulling apart complex puzzles, or simply contemplating things about life with a slew of friends specially created or modified to deal with my constant attempt to understand the world around me and inside me.

My friends were not even entirely invisible. As a child, I had a bedroom full of stuffed animals. Every one of them had a name and a personality. When a new one was brought home, I took out every single last one of those stuffed animals to introduce them to their new neighbor. I did this with so much believability that one could think I believed them to be alive. Truth be told, with all the living/killer toy movies I saw as a kid, it wouldn't have been a shock. However, that wasn't the case. I was just heavily engaged in a certain level of imaginative play. I knew they were just toys and I never really talked to them outside of a play session.

As an adult, I have more companions than I've ever had. I still daydream with characters of my creation and those of the creation of others. I still have long visits and adventures with them. Some are just to pass the time, some are to try and figure out life, some are to find a way to cope and deal with my troubles or contain my rage, and some are expressly left free-floating to form into what become new stories for me to write, tell, and publish. On the rare occasion, I create a character for outward entertainment, as is the case for my puppets. The presence of these characters in my life are extremely important to me and how I function through my days. Not only do they entertain me, but they entertain others as well.

My companions have also influenced me to learn new things. I designed a character for one of my novels. His hobby randomly became that he collected flags from all over the world. That same year, I too became curious and also began to collect flags from around the world. I had created a character for a short story that was supposed to paint matryoshka dolls. While I, at the time of this writing, have not painted my own, I've collected a few matryoshka dolls that have made their way to my bookshelf from their Russian origins. I love

German characters of both my creation and the creation of others and have since tried to learn the language. Two novels planned to be set in Russia inspired me to study Russian fairy tales and the Soviet Union in small Russian villages in the 1980s. I've learned how to make papyrus paper, I once learned how to write, to a degree in Egyptian hieroglyphs. I've studied several mythologies and took an interest in monsters and fairies of folklore. I've even learned how the different types of pearls are cultured, all because I wanted to become closer to the characters I enjoyed, created, and/or was in the process of creating. Some were for those storybooks I wanted to write. Some were just characters to daydream about while going about my day.

They Are Important to Me

Like the volunteers in my study, my creative companions were and are important to me and my development as a human being as my life continues to go on. My interests and curiosities will continue to be influenced by the multitude that appear.

My companions serve many functions. Some are simple, as I have mentioned before. They are there to be pawns of storytelling. Some sit with me either in my personal "real life space" and ponder great complexities with me, or muddle through mood swings with me in my internal imaginary world. My mood swings, as severe as they can be, can sometimes be lessened by actively interacting internally with these companions. On particularly serious ones (for good or bad), I may interact somewhat vocally to allow more decompression. Creative thinking is obviously not an issue for the likes of me.

That does bring up the question of social improvements. I suffer from depression, anxiety, and bi-polar disorder. I generally don't like public interaction, but I have learned to interact fine on a small scale. Granted, not everyone with a similar condition will have similar severities. While I'm not a social butterfly by any means, I can hold conversations with the right types of people and interact on a level of civility most of the time. I contribute this not only to necessity, but because I internally practice these scenarios with the wide range of characters and their personalities. It's not a perfect experience either in either interactions (real and imagined), but it does help to an extent. Some characters are just perfectly designed to brighten my mood when I need it and fight off the most severe of negative thoughts outside my control. Ironically, even some of the companion interactions are beyond my control. Or, to put it more clearly, I've worked my mind so much over my life that I can only suppose that my subconscious kicks into gear without my conscious effort to invoke certain types of companions.

I could argue that interactions with my creative companions internally have brought a little more awareness to empathy in others. The level of success is mediocre, at best. While I can exhibit some levels of empathy, I am still an oblivious person with major social awkwardness. While I don't always know how to interact or how oblivious I can sometimes unintentionally be, I do recognize that people will feel things in certain situations. Using creative companions rather than real people to think about these things allows me to still see those people as people, and it isn't as dramatic to make mistakes with an imagined companion while going through scenarios and exercises.

In essence, I would say that my creative companions continue to help mold me into an ever-changing complex human being. Even I don't always know the extent and I'm always along for the journey. Sometimes, it's good and sometimes it's not so good. Overall, I consider my experience with my companions as an integral part of my existence and my ability to acknowledge and interact with others. Where my health conditions (mental and physical) fail me, my ability to utilize my creative companions makes coping with those things a little bit easier. To be honest, I have no idea how I'd be able to function without them and the simple and complex methods of utilizations for which they are often used.

The Research

Being a topic that affects me in some manner, and one that I've seen little research in otherwise, I just had to find what I could about the idea of teens and adults having imaginary friends/creative companions. Surely, I was not the only adult to have them. Surely, I was not the only teenager to have them. There had to be others out there that were like me to some extent.

The research was a small scale one. The study pool was small, containing only a handful of volunteers. The time span was a mere fifteen weeks total, with only ten of them used for actual research and composition. However, even for such a small scale study, I feel that I've come to better understand how teens and adult utilize their own creative companions and to what capacity. As I expected, I am not the only person with these sorts of companions.

Also, I had a desperate desire to prove that creative companions were very natural and common among teens and adults, especially those of the creative sort. I wanted to dispel the notion that those with these companions, in any capacity, were, to use a broad layman term, *crazy*. The very idea of working with the topic of imaginary friends immediately brought up the snubs and offensive offhanded comments that I'd be working with people who "are crazy," or "should be locked away in a looney bin," or even "people who need to be on drugs." These statements seemed to totally ignore the fact that any of their closest friends or relatives or colleagues could very well have creative companions and live normal lives beside them. While some of those with creative companions may need medications to treat anxiety, depression, bi-polar disorder, or some form of autism, it's unfair to make the need for medications synonymous with "hallucinating things." In reality, those with creative companions are not hallucinating at all and actively and willingly create these companions. Not only do they create them, but are fully aware of their imaginative status. As the study shows, one does not need to be "crazy" or "schizophrenic" in order to have these companions. If anything, those with the more "negative" conditions have a very different relationship with the personalities and companions associated with their illnesses. As such, they are a symptom, not a therapy. In the case of those with imaginary friends who suffer from autism, anxiety, depression, and bi-polar disorder, they are more of a self-treatment, and a form of constant self-therapy; not a symptom, but a positive mental exercise.

Of course, more about this will be explained herein. It is the hope that this study will help to make readers more aware of the importance of creative companions and their utilizations. Misconceptions and misinformation can hopefully be cleared up. It is also the hope that, for those readers who have creative companions already can feel a sense of relief and validation that using one's imagination in this way is not necessarily something to be ashamed of or be concerned about, so long as their companions themselves do not become a negative aspect of their existence.

Imaginary Friends: Not Just Kid Stuff

When one mentions the idea of imaginary friends, there are two places the mind will commonly go. On the one hand, many associate the phenomenon with young children and the exploration of pretend play. These days, very little concern is placed on this common exhibition of child psychology. However, when the topic of imaginary friends is associated with those who are in their adolescence and adulthood, the negative outlook becomes quite apparent. The general public idea, as well as the idea presented by the media, by way of films and television shows, perpetuate the idea that imaginary friends in non-child individuals is an automatic sign of a dangerous psychosis and, in a layman's way of thinking, a type of lunacy. This shows little understanding or regard for the truth of the matter.

Herein, we can examine the commonality of the imaginary friend in adolescents and adults, but also show that this is not merely a symptom of psychosis. If anything, the more common usage for this companionship is to serve as a form of entertainment, social keys, and self-therapy, among other positive usages in which psychosis is not even considered nor present. Also, the types of companions created can be thereby extended into greater forms of creative thinking, such as puppeteers, role players, writers, and other such creators that make legitimate careers from the creation of imaginary companions.

It is duly noted that the concept of imaginary friends can even extend into the realm of spiritualism and religion. While literature and practical studies can tell us a lot about the types and usage of imaginary companions, it is equally unfair to consider religious entities in this realm. While the argument can be present, the idea of imaginary companions in adolescents and adults primarily, in this case, relies on the fact that the creators are aware these companions are indeed imaginary. To place religious entities under such a category would be unfair and offensive. Thereby, herein, the concept of gods, angels, devils, etc. are of no consideration, as it cannot be unanimously accepted by others and the "creators" that these are accepted as fictional entities.

It is with great purpose to show that imaginary friends are not subject to just small children. It is also with great purpose to show that the garnered stigmatic view of the concept is contrary to the actual truth of the purpose and utilization of such things. Imaginary friends are not only present in adolescents and adults, but can also be hypothesized as common, normal, and healthy, separate from the misconceptions of serious psychotic disorders in which such are seen as symptomatic rather than therapeutic. As it stands, it can be firmly suspect that there is more to this phenomenon than laymen and some experts dare to give the proper credit.

In a nutshell, the purpose of the imaginary friend in adolescent and adults will be explored. What are the stigmas that are often faced? What are the benefits, if any? Of course, it's also important that herein, we discover the different types of companions, as the usage and stigmas applies could vary from type to type. Above all, it the phenomenon in these age group common, and if they are, are they healthy?

Literature Review

Misconceptions & Stereotypes

One thing is for certain, and that's that the idea of imaginary friends is stigmatized. Many do not understand the full scope or function of these entities. When the notion comes to mind, people associate this with mental illness, bringing to mind levels of insanity and instability. Images of PolyGram Filmed Entertainment's 1991 film *Drop Dead Fred* often come to mind.

In the film, the main character, Elizabeth, gains an imaginary friend (Drop Dead Fred, played by the late Rik Mayall) as a child to deal with her overbearing mother. When her life falls apart as an adult, Fred returns to wreak havoc on her life, making her appear visibly insane until she learns to face and cope with her troubles. Surely, for the common person, this is an idea that would stick around in association with the term "imaginary friend." It's no wonder then that many adolescents and adults do not openly discuss their experiences with such entities. However, this idea of the imaginary friend can also misconstrue what these entities actually are and how they are used for others. The phenomenon, when all possible definitions and theories are combined, are quite common by comparison to what society portrays, as will be explained in further detail.

It should be no surprise then that early studies of the imaginary friend phenomenon were less than encouraging. Some of the most common misconceptions regarding imaginary friends in the medical/psychological field stated that these entities were a sign of dissociative disorder (DID)/multiple personality disorder or schizophrenia (Lydon, 2011). While this isn't entirely false, it's also not entirely true. A lot of factors were overlooked or ignored entirely in favor of a result stating that imaginary friends were created as defense mechanisms for trauma in children (Lydon, 2011). It should also be no surprise that a stigma of imaginary friends shows a lack of social skills, and that the individuals with these companions are somehow unable to discern fantasy from reality (Jean Piaget Society, 2007). The idea that individuals are somehow unable to tell that their companions or situations are fictional is generally false. If anything, individuals describe their imaginary companions as "a different sort of real" and are well aware these companions are entirely pretend or real in a different sense (The Genius Experiment, 2014).

As far as stigmas are concerned, it would be wise to consider factors such as: religion, culture, background, location, etc. The perception of imaginary friends may indicate different things to outsiders (most notably being parents). For example, one study done on children in Mexico and the

United States showed that the U.S subjects with imaginary friends were met with a lot more acceptance. However, ¼ of the subjects from Mexico were perceived to have a propensity for lying when the topic of imaginary friends arose (Jean Piaget Society, 2007). It is safe to assume that, in the face of these stigmas, those individuals with imaginary companions may sometimes become reserved or secretive about their companions in the face of others. It's fair to say, therefore, that those with imaginary companions are easily made aware of the stigmas facing them. Roblyer (2014) stated in his lecture, *Adults Need More Imaginary Friends* that it is unacceptable for adults to talk to entities that are non-existent the way children do and that adults tend to face harsher labels and stigmas than those that face children (2:50). He adds jokingly, "When a grown man stands in front of you and says he talks to people that don't exist, there are generally two reactions. One is that people will nod and back away slowly. The other is to assume this man is an artist of some kind…then nod and back away as fast as possible" (Roblyer, 2014, 1:59).

Imaginary companions in adolescents and adults is not only generally common in one respect or another, but there is a long history of imaginary companions being created and kept by many great minds. One of the earliest examples is Socrates. In his time, the phenomenon of an imaginary friends referred to as a person's "genius" and was thought of as a guardian spirit. Everyone was thought to have at least one, and they were responsible for providing most creative insight (The Genius Experiment, 2014). It was believed that these entities could bestow or invoke a great deal of wisdom. This idea resurfaced in the 1940s, as researchers started to show a new sense of interest in this topic within the psychodynamic tradition. The idea of imaginary companionship was discussed as the superego, the ego and the id concepts in psychoanalytic (Dissertation Planet, 2014). Other notable names of infamous adults with imaginary companions include:

Eleanor Roosevelt, Sir Isaac Newton, the infamous Bronte siblings (Branwell, Anna, Charlotte, and Emily), and Machiavelli, just to name a few (The Genius Experiment, 2014; Root-Bernstein, 2008; Sherman, 2013).

One thing that many experts would agree on is that imaginary companions serve a function. This is regardless of when they appear, be it in childhood, adolescence, or adulthood. The influence and practices utilized among these companions can serve as a healthy tool for many of the individuals with them, or general majority.

Imaginary Friends in Childhood

While certainly not the focus of the study, it would be unwise to ignore the importance and prevalence of childhood and the role of imaginary companions therein. It is, after all, the most notable and popular time for individuals to experience the phenomenon. Unlike the theories of mental disorders and trauma, recent studies (those relating to creative play/thinking, development, and personal speech) have found that the presence of imaginary companions are beneficiary and healthy in the development of children (Connor, 2005; Davis et al, 2013; The Genius Experiment, 2014; Honeycut et al, 2013; Jean Piaget Society, 2007; Lydon, 2011; Root-Bernstain, 2008).

Rather than loneliness, these companions appear spontaneously in order for the child to play, experiment, and express in a means that is under their control with little to no consequence to the child's regular social existence (Honeycutt et al, 2013). In other words, children with imaginary friends tend to have them out of boredom and exploration, yet still maintain a number of real life friends and social interactions as well (The Genius Experiment, 2014; Grodinsky, 2015; Jean Piaget Society, 2007). In fact, the presence of an imaginary companion is thought to improve the social, cognitive, and creative thinking process in the child, allowing for greater creative play and socialization with others (Connor, 2005). Other skills to be gained from these interactions include speech development, cognitive thinking, and allowing a child to understand perspective and empathy (Davis et al, 2013; Kidd, 2012).

The important part to take into consideration is the process of creativity in play for experimentation and allowing a child to create an identity (Honeycutt et al, 2013). Evan Kidd (2012) stated that pretend play requires creative thinking and sequencing of events. Therefore, those engaged with pretend play via engaging with an imaginary companion, are more frequently utilizing this skill.

While 60-70% of young children are estimated to have at least one imaginary companion in some scope, these companions can appear and vanish spontaneously (Connor, 2005). While many children lose their imaginary friends over time, others are able to maintain, replace, or create new ones throughout their lives. Every single one allows the individual some sort of expression. As Roblyer (2012) said in his lecture, "Imaginary friends are not trivial, regardless of how long they stick around" (6:35).

Imaginary Friends in Adolescents and Adults

Kidd (2012) stated in his lecture, *Imaginary Friends*, that play and pleasure are important for combatting anxiety and depression. As a child moves onto adolescents and adulthood, less focus is put on play and more on academic focus and practical tasks, often leading to an absence of the ability to express creativity.

Adolescents have been known to write to imaginary companions in their diaries. It has also been shown that they create and maintain imaginary companions even to simply alleviate boredom (Jean Piaget Society, 2007). Even with imaginary friends, whether they openly admit to having them or not, it is understood that these companions do not ultimately replace or stand in lieu of real friends and social interactions. It is theorized that the companions function much in the same way that they do in children, though made to fit the situations of the adolescent life (Jean Piaget Society, 2007).

Adults are also prone to creating imaginary companions. While many cases would be in similar fashion to that of adolescents, focused on the topics adults would face, there are some professions in which imaginary companions are not only common, but even encouraged (Jean Piaget Society, 20070). The most common example is that of the writer. Creating characters is expected and often given a lot of "life," via the illusion of independent agency. *The illusion of independent agency* is defined as "when a character is created by a writer but has its own autonomy outside the control of the author" (Jean Piaget Society, 2007).

A good example of how characters created can grow would be to examine the lives of the Bronte siblings. In the 19th century, these siblings spent their childhood playing with toys and creating elaborate stories about their imaginary world. As they grew older, they elaborated further with new towns and characters and events. These characters were such a part of their lives that they allowed the siblings, not only to present mature thought at an early age, but provided the stories they later wrote into novels, "laying the foundation for 19th century literature" (Root-Bernstein, 2008).

Individuals of any age can have imaginary companions to some degree. It extends in the adult realm even beyond that of authors, depending on the intended purpose. It should be noted that these companions are understood to be just that: imaginary by the individual in question. That being said, we should examine some of the different *types* of imaginary friends that are utilized.

Types of Imaginary Companions

There are many different types of imaginary companions that anyone of any age can have. Not only does it include a "separate" entity, but also an alternate version of oneself, for lack of a better term, a doppelgänger. Regardless of the form, they all fall under the category of imaginary companion and serve as the like.

The most commonly recognized form of imaginary friend is the "invisible friend." This type is created entirely by an individual's imagination and cannot be seen by others. The appearance of these invisible friends can vary to any degree. Some can be really scary while others can look quite silly. It's estimated that 60% of imaginary friends are human in nature while 40% are animal in some way (Connor, 2005). These entities can also manifest, not just as made up people/creatures, but perhaps even actual entities, such as passed on loved ones.

Another common manifestation of imaginary companions is that of personification. This manifestation involves sentience being applied to an object, such as a stuffed animal, a doll, a toy, or some random object (Lydon, 2011). A popular example of this form of imaginary companionship would be the *Calvin & Hobbes* comics, in which, to Calvin, Hobbes is a real tiger companion with whom to go on adventures. However, in reality, he's simply a plush tiger (Jean Piaget Society, 2007).

A somewhat unspoken manifestation of imaginary companionship is that of parasocial relationships. A parasocial relationship is a fictional friendship, relationship, or closeness to anyone or anything ranging from celebrities to fictional characters in books, movies, or television. While this can involve a lot of real, existing people, there is a general level of logic applied to these relationships to denote them as fantasy (Barnes, 2016). In a world full of stimulating media, individuals can engage in closeness with their chosen companion in the imaginary sense. Jennifer Barnes (2016), in her lecture, *Imaginary Friends and Real World Consequences: Parasocial Relationships*, adamantly stated "Logically, we know fictional characters do not exist and do not know us. Logically, we know celebrities have millions of fans and do not know us personally even though it sometimes feels like we do" (5:26). She goes on to explain that one's investment in these characters or celebrities stems from what is called *alief*. Alief is defined as "an automatic, gut-level, belief-like attitude that may contradict a specifically held belief" (Barnes, 2016, 5:50). Her example was that of someone in a glass elevator flying over the town. Logically, one would know that this elevator is safe, while the alief response still considers there to be the danger of falling. In that aspect, though one logically knows the relationship is make believe and friendships are not real, the alief reaction still manages to convince the individual of that closeness (Barnes, 2016).

Another form of imaginary friend is the *–sona* or *Fandom-sona*. This falls more under the category of doppelgänger, in which an individual is able to create an imaginary version of themselves in order to explore creative thought (Juliani, 2016). This form of imaginary expression can easily coincide with other forms, as the –sona chosen can be entirely made up or inspired by fictional sources. Examples of this are such things as the *fursona* for those in the furry community, in which they have an anthropomorphic animal form, a *pony-sona* in regards to the *My Little Pony: Friendship is Magic* fandom, in which the person envisions themselves as a pony character (or other related species in the show, such as griffons or dragons). One could also have a *monster-sona* in regards to a fandom for the PC game *Undertale*, or a *gemsona* in regards to the *Steven Universe* fandom, in which characters are personified gems. Those are simply a few examples of this doppelgänger form of imaginary play.

The last form of imaginary companion to be discussed is that of the *tulpa*. The literal translation for tulpa from Tibetan is "thought form" (Stewart, 2016). Samuel Veissiere (2015) describes them as "imaginary companions who are said to have achieved full sentience after being conjured through 'thought-form' meditative practice. Human 'hosts', or tulpamancers, mediate their practice through open-ended how-to guides and discussion forums on the Internet and experience their tulpas as semi-permanent auditory and somatic hallucinations." This was an ancient practice by Tibetan Buddhist monks in order to connect with their deities.

In modern culture, tulpamancy is seen less as a spiritual cause and more as a form of creating companionship. The general statistics of tulpamancers are adolescents and young adult males who feel a sense of loneliness or social awkwardness (Juliani, 2016). While there is no real change in the level of intelligence between tulpamancers and those with or without more traditional imaginary companions, the inadequacies are in contrast. That being said, many tulpamancers still utilize their tulpas in the same manner as others use more traditional imaginary companions. Many tulpamancers have claimed to have suffered a great deal of anxiety, depression, or autism and feel adamant about the idea of their tulpas making them better to some degree, as well as more empathic and aware of others around them (Juliani, 2016; Stewart, 2016).

Similar to the Fandom-sona and parasocial relationships, the tulpa can also draw on other fictional or inspired means, like celebrities, superheroes, TV shows, movies, and books. There have been accounts of people, animals, "furry" and "pony" tulpas being thought into creation, as well as any number of other characters, original or not, from fandoms becoming the chosen form of the individual's tulpa (Veissiere, 2015).

Review Summary

In conclusion, it becomes apparent that, overall, imaginary companions are quite common and healthy to, not just children, but individuals of any age. This does not entirely exclude or debunk that such manifestations *can* appear in the mentally ill, but it certainly isn't the general rule of thumb. These companions allow individuals to explore fears, anger, identity, and general mental stimulation (alleviating boredom). They also provide a chance to practice cognitive and creative thinking and social role play.

Despite the stigmas and stereotypes about imaginary interactions present due to media dramatizations and ignorance, these companions are common, functional, and considered a healthy part of development, coping, stress relief, and, to many, an integral part of the creative process.

Methodology

It is important to not look exclusively at the research of others. In order to get a better look at how these imaginative entities or creative companions are utilized, it is important to explore how these entities affect people first hand. Such a straightforward approach would offer the ability to observe if the results are supplementary, in agreement with, or contrary to the studies presented in the literature depicting previous studies.

A great deal of the literature, while touching on adolescents and adults, primarily focus on small children. While the information obtained by *those* studies are certainly insightful in the use of creative companionship in older individuals, there is a general lack of personal experience from adolescents and adults with imaginary companions (in some capacity) documented. It is important to therefore document some of these experiences to add a human element to the study itself, rather than abstract the participants merely as soulless subjects. While the volunteers will have aliases throughout the study, they are still presenting their personal experiences. Also, in consideration of their personal experiences, the term *imaginary friends* will henceforth be known as *creative companionship*.

In order to conduct this study, 12 volunteers will be selected and interviewed about their experience with their creative companions and to what capacity. They will also get to share the reasoning behind creating these companions or imaginative alter-egos. When it comes to locating these volunteers, an alert will be placed on social media with contact information. It is the hope that volunteers with a variety of creative companionship experiences will apply. This would allow for a more intriguing exploration of the experiences and how they both relate and differ from one another. Volunteers will also be interviewed on the matter of any personal stigmas they have or currently face when it comes to their creative companionships. These volunteers will also vary in age and will include both adolescents and adults (primarily each volunteer, to qualify for this study much be aged 14 or older). As stated previously, to protect their identities, they will be given aliases. Special precautions have also been considered in the cases of minors needing consent of their parents or guardians. This consent allowed minor volunteers to participate in the interview, but that the parent/guardian would not be present for said interview. It is a priority to protect the privacy and trust of adolescent volunteers, even from their own families, while still managing to inform parents/guardians of the nature of the study. This is due to the awareness that exposing the study too simply could result in undesirable consequences of adolescent volunteers. Wording must be done with the utmost of care for the sake of those adolescent volunteers.

The hypothesis is that, despite what stigmas would imply, these adolescents are not only fully aware of the imaginative state of their companions, but also utilize them in a multitude of positive ways. Some of these ways will likely include: alleviating boredom/daydreaming, a method of venting frustrations, creative therapeutic means, fictional world exploration through imagination or role playing, internal practice of social skills, and world *building* through creative storytelling, to state a few. It is also hypothesized that significant mental illnesses will not be present among the volunteers. More specifically, dire mental illnesses such as dissociative identity disorder (DID) or schizophrenia. However, this does not include "milder" disorders. It is hypothesized that there are likely going to be volunteers who do suffer from anxiety, depression, and perhaps Asperger's syndrome, though allowing volunteers with these afflictions over others still shows a level of functionality in the individual. In essence, those with the "milder" afflictions are capable of being fully aware of the imaginative status of their companions and a level of control over said entities.

It is the purpose to show that creative companions are not signs of insanity or instability. On the contrary, it is hypothesized that these creative companions serve a very positive and/or important role in the lives of generally normal and functioning adolescents and adults.

Data Collection

The Research Method and Guidelines

In accordance to the methodology plan, announcements were placed, via social media centers, such as Tumblr, Facebook, and Twitter. Potential volunteers were instructed to send a private message in order to be screened for the process. The limitations were few but strict. In essence, one could not participate without any form of creative companion (a term surprisingly a lot looser in its definition than originally expected), and an absence of dissociative identity disorder (DID) and/or schizophrenia. As for DID, no such cases arose, though several volunteers had to be turned away due to having a schizophrenia diagnosis, regardless of how aware and under control the condition was being treated. That being said, other conditions were allowed in order to research some aspects of creative companions in adolescents and adults (a curiosity of development, cause and effect). These conditions primarily were narrowed down to forms of anxiety, depression, bi-polar disorder, and high functioning autism (formerly known as Asperger's Syndrome).

While the questions asked were designed to gather as much information for consideration as possible, several aspects were not covered due to the time and social constraints present. As such, race was not heavily considered (though upbringing was, which could include racial heritage, but was not defined solely as such). Other factors that were not considered opened up possibilities of perceived (or actual) abusive situations, a heavier focus on social standing, the number of siblings and the birth order of those siblings, sexualities, familial taboos, locations both past and present, and education, among other such constructs. For a more effective set of results, with those concepts added, one would need a much larger pool of a menagerie of volunteers to fill all those requirements for a study of results of those areas. As such, the interviews focused primarily on the companions themselves, the motivation, benefit, negative experiences and purpose of those companions.

The Volunteers

Twelve volunteers were chosen. The interviews were done via Skype call after consent forms were sent and returned. Volunteers were given the opportunity to ask questions and voice any confusion or concern, not just before or after the interview, but during. After understandable initial nervousness, the volunteers opened up rather quickly to share their experiences.

Upon review of the information gathered, all twelve volunteers were given an alias. These aliases were created based on some facet of the individual being interviewed or a facet of one of the characters of which they shared. All aliases are preceded by *S*, as in *Subject*, and after which, the alias. The aliases are as follows, in no particular order: 1. *S-France* 2. *S-London* 3. *S-Moscow* 4. *S-Delaware* 5. *S-Sugar* 6. *S-Tibet* 7. *S-Lilypad* 8. *S-Bunny* 9. *S-JJ* 10. *S-Dragon* 11. *S-Frankie* and 12. *S-Aqua*. They ranged from 17-33 years of age. Many of these volunteers had multiple companions as well, each one serving different purposes or different purposes within a purpose. Among those with many, there was always at least one of special significance or importance. Volunteers also varied in gender, with 7 identifying as female, 4 as male, and one as gender-fluid. Of them, ¾ identified as being religious to some degree, most identifying as Christian, Catholic, or Agnostic, with ¼ being Atheist.

After reviewing the transcripts of the interviews, it was discovered that seven of the twelve volunteers suffered from one or more of the acceptable conditions. Three of those with conditions were diagnosed with autism. The majority primarily held diagnoses for anxiety and depression, with only one mentioning bi-polar disorder. The information showed that there were definitely social obstacles with most of them, admittedly.

Creative Companion Construct

To review, the creative companions covered a broad range of aspects. The typical "imaginary friend" or "invisible friend" was indeed included, as are the other concepts in the realm of child psychology (child, in this case, being defined as anyone under the age of 14), such as: personified objects, alter-egos or some type of –sona. Also included were tulpas, parasocial friendships (fictional characters and real people alike), original characters (OCs), fictional characters (self-taking of existing fictional characters or creating of new ones for storytelling purposes), symbolic or personifications of specific feelings, concepts, and places, and puppets (such as hand puppets, marionettes, and ventriloquist figures).

Negativity and Stigmas

Obviously, the first concern to come to mind is the effect of these creative companions on those who have them in relation to self and the public. 2/3 of the volunteers experienced some form of negativity or stigma due to having their creative companions. This is regardless of the type of companion created. On the bright side, of those volunteers, the negativity was mild. Most issues stemmed from character design or personality. For those that identify as role players, there have been the occasional issue of a rude player in their community. Again, the complaints are often due to the difference of creative presentation and choice. Anyone in a creative field could expect such a thing. That isn't to say that public negativity wasn't present. Aside from the disagreement of character design/personality/presentation, there was no other negativity. *S-Lilypad, S-Delaware,* and *S-Aqua* have admitted to getting negative comments and perceptions from others who have found out about their companions. Both *S-Lilypad* and *S-Aqua* have admitted, "People find it weird. They think I'm crazy and need psychological help." In the case of *S-Delaware*, her experience was "Despite my hard work and excellence in everything that I do, people find it childish and immature. They liken it with a denial of growing up and an inability to tell the difference between fantasy and reality." Negativity in the case of *S-Bunny*, however, was more of a personal strike. "I sometimes have trouble balancing the fantasy and reality" they said, not to be confused with the inability to decipher such. "I feel childish and irresponsible or immature." Nothing else in their interview suggested that this was the factual case, but the illogical perception of *S-Bunny* from time to time, normally during times of poor moods.

Expressions of Creativity

It's clear that there are a lot of creative minds among the volunteers. Most identify as writers and authors to some degree, be it in comics, fanfiction, role playing, or writing books. If one was to step outside of the intricate slew of fictional characters created simply for storytelling, we would still be left with a few interesting volunteers. One, *S-Tibet*, was the only one to primarily discuss the presence and function of tulpas. He named and described three as well as the circumstances for their creation, ranging from curiosity to a series of life events that somehow triggered either his own desire or the desire of the other tulpas to have companions. Tulpas differ slightly from what one would perceive as an "imaginary friend" in the stereotypical sense, as tulpas are perceived to be in a plain of actual existence, even if not visible. There were a few other volunteers who admitted to having a fursona, which serve as both a separate entity from the creator (therefor a companion) but also a sort of expression of the self of that creator (therefore a –sona). This is the case for volunteers *S-Frankie, S-Bunny,* and *S-Sugar*. While all three have other creative companions for other creative purposes, the fursona is a way to express a certain side of the self and create a form of identity. In the case of *S-Sugar*, she claimed that her fursona, a rabbit/bat hybrid was a companion of hers throughout adolescence. "I created her when I was 13, and she's changed her shape, but she is still a fun character," she said. *S-Frankie* has described her fursona, a Dumbo rat, as a part of herself, but also her own entity; she became something that allowed her to experiment with a fascination as well as bring her into a community of other people with similar interest, therefore creating new friendships. *S-Bunny* has the most prominent fursona in the sense of the –sona being a piece of them and less of a separate entity. *S-Bunny* has identified good naturedly as the fursona, with gleeful "I'm the bunny" type comments. To be clear, *S-Bunny* has not confused themselves with the -sona, but simply considers the fursona an extension of themselves. This is also true of another of *S-Bunny*'s creations. This volunteer presented themselves as gender-fluid. As biological gender is not a major focus in the study, it was interesting to see how this volunteer laid out their companions or –sonas, or even what one could call the alter-ego. They mentioned the existence of Delilah as the female version of themselves to play against the male body. In essence, Delilah is just as much of an existing force as *S-Bunny*'s biological experience, as they can live interchangeably as one being. While a complex notion, it does still fall under the category of creative companions, for this version of *self* had to be realized and formed into that which *S-Bunny* lives.

S-Frankie also displayed parasocial friendship. While other volunteers had characters of whom they were attached that belonged to someone else (*S-Sugar*'s characters being inspired by characters created by Toby Fox for his computer game, *Undertale*, for example), *S-Frankie*'s fan favorite character has been described as being "adopted" by her and a companion she holds very near and dear. The character, of whom she named Adam, is the monster created by Dr. Frankenstein in Mary

Shelley's *Frankenstein*. Having a major connection to the character and disliking the media portrayal of him, she bestowed a name on him and made him her own, so to speak. This parasocial friendship is a very strong one, even by her own admittance.

The Role Play Character

The most common trait among the volunteers was the creation of what started out as or eventually evolved into role playing characters. These characters were placed into online role playing communities via forums or social media for character experimentation and social development. As such, all volunteers with role playing characters (including OCs) have admitted seeing an increase in their social skills, as well as an increase in the number of people in their social circles. To be fair, not all volunteers were role players. Many identified as writers to some extent and artists. *S-JJ* stood out the most, having connections to characters created for comic books. His characters, he said, were to represent aspects of himself. These aspects consisted not just of personality, but also of his views of perfection, his ability to express different levels of masculinity and femininity, exploring his love of superheroes, and also indulging in certain kinks and taboos that are (perhaps until recently) often not present in the corporate comic book world. Similar can be said of *S-London*, who claimed to create his character as a form of arousing fantasies, fetish exploration, and levels of storytelling.

S-JJ is also not the only volunteer to personify a self aspect. Though while he is able to explore possibilities with these characters, others use such companions in a more therapeutic way or in a way to help simplify complicated constructs. Such is the case with *S-Sugar* and *S-Dragon*, and perhaps to a lesser extent, *S-Delaware*. For example, *S-Dragon* has created companions to personify complicated constructs and, as he put it "personifying or symbolizing a name or phrase." As for the *why* of this practice, one can only hypothesize as there is no definite answer. In the case of *S-Sugar*, the companions are more directly linked to feelings and behaviors: symbolic, realized, or manipulated. Her experience revolves around two companions created to work as a Jekyll and Hyde construct. "Sugar," she said, referring to one of her companions "is the character that makes me happy. When I think of him, I am inspired to do art or be playful. Even if I'm not particularly happy, I can use him to make me happy." Likewise, the counterpart companion, known as Sour, is very similar a character and while it doesn't particularly provide a therapeutic or useful nature in the same way as Sugar, she stated, "If I start to use him, people who are familiar with the characters get the idea pretty quick that all is not well and happy." As for *S-Delaware*, her companion is the personification of her state (as well as other similar characters of hers). This character allows her to explore and experience history and view new perspectives while encouraging her need and desire for constant research and learning. He (her character), personifies her defiance, her eagerness to learn, her silliness, and many other aspects of her personality and pride.

The Results and the Literature

The results of the study seem to agree with the literary sources and expand on the insight of adolescents and adults with these companions and their uses. It's not a phenomenon specific to young children. It is not only prevalent in adults, but serve a great deal of positive purposes. There is a common theme among the volunteers for both purposeful and random forms of creating storytelling. As such, they develop their own imagination as well social skills when that creativity is applied to others in a community (Kidd, 2012; Roblyer 2014). Due to the types and uses of these creative companions, it's also safe to say that this is a more common occurrence than people would want to believe. It's not limited to "invisible friends" but a slew of creative characters manifested in many different ways. Those ways seem to be relieving boredom, but not necessarily loneliness, but a form of entertainment

Companions are created for the specific purpose of exploration of ideas, storytelling, art, and joining a community, and therefore encouraging social skills. These are all consistent with the literary findings as suggested by Juliani (2016) and Stewart (2016). Specifically, the companions of the volunteers have managed to create and show improvements to varying degrees in relation to the social anxieties and awkwardness of their creators. The disorders considered also show that the companions are not a symptom of those conditions, but a coping mechanism and treatment plan/therapy for those with them. It should also be noted that relying on an absence of DID and schizophrenia, the concept of imaginary friends on any level is not necessarily a negative symptom of a serious mental disorders or traumatic experiences, as suggested by early psychologists (Lyndon 2011). If anything, the results show a positive level of self-treatment against the symptoms of the cause, rather than the companions themselves being manifestations *of* the cause and thereby being, in themselves, the symptom. For example, the companions created served to create a means for social interaction in some form, despite the volunteer's social anxieties. The companions have also allowed a form of joy in those with depression. The companions created have put their creators in a place that was better off than the place they were beforehand.

All twelve volunteers have admitted to seeing improvements of some sort to their lives with the presence of their creative companions. They all take entertainment from their companions. Social skills have improved, new friendships were formed, and many developments arose, such as empathy, patience, the ability to see new perspectives, to name a few. There was also an improvement in creative thinking, writing skills, refreshing the usage of imagination and inspiration, art skills, and, in the case of *S-JJ*, monetary gain. One could then probably safely assume that creative companions are common, a part of the human experience, regardless of age, serve a purpose or multiple purposes, and are an overall positive and welcome experience to those who have them.

5

Final Thoughts

According to the literature and volunteer study alike, it is apparent that creative companions are a very common and beneficial part of the human experience, at least in the realm of creativity and self-therapy. One can obviously not ignore that there are times when such companionship is a negative symptom of greater psychoses, such as DID and schizophrenia. No study, as of current, can erase that these occurrences can and do happen. What we can learn, however, is that the experience of creative companions is not exclusive to these psychoses and do not exclusively pose a negative influence. To have a creative companion, to any capacity/manifestation, for any reason, is not an automatic sign of such diagnoses. However, this being the case, it is hard to see the common practice and beneficial influence in the mainstream, not just in media alone, but even in the realm of psychological/psychiatric practice.

For example, one instance of a letter writer (LW) to a doctor describes an account of what Barnes called the *parasocial relationship* (2015). In this case, it involved that of a real, yet deceased individual: Freddie Mercury (Randal, 2013). LW described her encounters with this entity and the close friendship. One could expect that the *alief* concept would be at work here. More specifically, it could lead the reader to wonder if LW is aware that Freddie Mercury is not her personal friend, but also deceased. According to the letter, this is not the case, and LW is fully aware that her friendship is imaginary, but draws a sense of joy and comfort therein. Dr. Kristina Randal replied to LW with "You perceive this 'imaginary friend' as being healthy but if it is not real, then it's unhealthy"

(2013). Considering ongoing studies and advocating for an aware interaction between individuals and their creative companions, Randal's response to LW definitely comes off as the misguided and hasty diagnosis and stigma those with creative companions could face, even from professionals who should know better.

To be fair, of the volunteers interviewed in the study, only a few experienced actual negativity due to stigma. The reactions of outsiders, regardless of the type of companion or the purpose, was certainly to be respected. Even setting up the study and research, many people referred to the concept as "crazy" and people needing to be in the "looney bin" for having companions, with no consideration for the type or purpose. The concept of creative thinking, self-therapy, and entertainment seemed to be a foreign concept.

It should be clear by now that creative companions are nothing "crazy" or "looney" when explored in a mature manner. Even some schools have programs that utilize the benefit of creative companions and imaginative interactions via role playing. In such a program, teachers take on the roles of literary characters and allow their students to communicate with said character, often showing a positive result in creative thinking and coping in those students (Andrews, 2015). According to the volunteer interviews, it is further displayed that creating these companions and utilizing them in writing, role playing, artwork, and even other forms of entertainment are done not to isolate themselves nor show a sense of shortcomings. In fact, the evidence displays the opposite, with these individuals vying for community and social interactions in an environment and setup that is comfortable and challenging, resulting in a somewhat better ability to create, think, and interact in their real lives. After all, one would not call J.K. Rowling "crazy" for writing a book full of developed characters. One would not refer to someone like Jeff Dunham as a "looney" for creating vibrant and creative characters in his ventriloquist act. These forms of companions *are* included under the category and often overlooked.

Imagination: Everyone is Guilty

Whether people want to admit it or not, they are guilty of creating a creative companion at some point for some purpose. Perhaps it's a fantasy or daydream. Perhaps scenarios play through the head of an individual to create proper problem solving. That being said, there is a slight divide among those who are realistically based and those who are creatively based. It is not to say either is more intelligent than the other. Intelligence isn't the case. For instance, Cynthia Jeub, owner of a blog called *Insights on Epic Living*. She describes herself as a person who grew up being imaginative, but with strict limitations on realism. "Everything had to be as close to real life as possible," she stated (Jeub, 2014, p.1). At the age of 21, she acquired a plush toy that became her creative companion. The purpose?

The plush companion was an experiment of her own after hearing the lecture of Roblyer and his take on imaginary friends in adults. It was something with imaginary sentience in which she could voice her concerns and thoughts. Jeub not only talks about the personal experience and how it helped her, but also the inclusion of virtual reality or imaginary worlds and people. As such, she expressed how hard it was to function when there was only reality and not enough virtual reality/imaginary reality (Jeub, 2014). As examples, she not only mentions characters in literature, but also media industries and the creation of video games.

On an interesting note, one author, Laura Diamond, briefly reflected on the phenomenon of personal characters and the generic creative companion. Dismissing the notion of a psychosis, such as DID and schizophrenia, Diamond noted that human beings, including adults, had a creative and social *need* for these companions (2016). She put aside the need of, what we could call, *professional level character creation* and acknowledged the more common forms of creative companions. The notion suggested was that creative companions can be linked to an *attachment theory* (Diamond, 2016). Bowlby's attachment theory more often refers to relationships between human beings. It's an interesting concept to think of this relationship and attachment as being just as plausible in those that are not physically real. In a nutshell, the theory states that a deep and emotional relationship can be formed from one person to another, regardless of space and time and does not necessarily have to be reciprocated (McLeod, 2009). While the theory primarily deals with the relationships between other human beings, primarily parent-child relationships, it can be said that such attachments, as it is defined, can fall into the realm of the role of creative companions in children and adults alike (Diamond, 2016; McLeod, 2009).

Insane or Natural?

It begs the question: is creativity in and of itself a sign of insanity, if we are to believe that creative companions are a sign of mental illness? Obviously, considering the entertainment business as it stands, that's obviously not quite the case. To be fair, the average person would point out those who are not using their creativity for outward creative gain (entertainment, profit, pretend world play in social circles, etc). Perhaps the idea of "craziness" is applied to those with –sonas, a complex imaginary world and imaginary inhabitants (the daydreamer), or the personification of objects as a physical outlet. Even then, this seems to be an unfair "diagnosis" from layman and professional alike. Few creators adamantly state their companions are as real as another human being. Importance and emotional bonds are prominent, but all those with creative companions are very aware of their imaginary status and different level of existence from other human beings. That is the purpose of imagination. While these companions may influence creative thinking and an ability to cope with issues in the real world, it's not common practice for these companions to have such control over their creators as to form negative influence. This is generally what separates those with the negative diagnoses (DID and schizophrenia) from those who are simply being creative to feel better in some form or fashion (Honeycut, et al, 2013).

Conclusion

Overall, it can be safely assumed that creative companions are common, not just in children, but in adolescents and adults for any number of given reasons and practices. Due to the type of functions those companions serve and the benefits that result from their presence, it's obviously a natural occurrence as well, as human beings, in essence are creative creatures by nature. It is also fair to say that, while social anxieties do seem prominent in many creators, introversion and anxiety are not prerequisites of creating companions. Creators are able to live perfectly normal lives with their companions. Age seems to be irrelevant. The older or more complex the individual, the more complex the companion may become. Likewise, the more involved within a community or fandom an individual may be, the more specific their companions may be, be they originally created or merely canon adoptions of existing characters. Without exposing them openly, many would never even know of the presence of such a companion in others. Indeed, the negativity against creators is unfair and unwarranted and the stigmas are misplaced. So long as creators are aware that their companions are their creations and are not negatively influenced by them, there is no need for the fear of one's mental stability.

RESOURCES

Andrew, J. (2015, April 3). Undercover teachers or imaginary friends? - The Atlantic. Retrieved from http://www.theatlantic.com/education/archive/2015/04/undercover-teachers-or-imaginary-friends/389649/

Barnes, J. (2015, March 2). *Imaginary friends and real-world consequences: Parasocial relationships | Jennifer Barnes at TEDxOU* [Video file]. Retrieved from https://www.youtube.com/watch?v=22yoaiLYb7M

Connor, M. J. (2005, November). Imaginary friends. Retrieved from http://www.mugsy.org/connor70.htm

Davis, P. E., Meins, E., & Fernyhough, C. (2013). Individual differences in children's private speech: The role of imaginary companions. *Journal of Experimental Child Psychology, 116*(3), 561-571. doi:10.1016/j.jecp.2013.06.010

Diamond, L. (2016, February 20). Mental health Monday–Imaginary friends…normal or not??? Retrieved from https://lbdiamond.wordpress.com/2012/02/20/mental-health-monday-imaginary-friends-normal-or-not/

Dissertation Planet. (2014). Creative personality: A result of imaginary companionship.

Retrieved from https://www.dissertationplanet.co.uk/creative-personality-result-imaginary-companionship/

The Genius Experiment. (2014, March). Imaginary friends: Why do children have imaginary friends? Retrieved from www.geniusexperiment.com/2014/03/imaginary-friends/

Grodinsky, L. (2015, January 5). How childhood imaginary companions shape our adult lives — NURJ. Retrieved from http://www.thenurj.com/how-childhood-imaginary-companions-shape-our-adult-lives/

Honeycutt, J. M., Pecchioni, L., Keaton, S. A., & Pence, M. E. (2013). Developmental implications of mental imagery in childhood imaginary companions. *Journal of Experimental Child Psychology, 116*(3), 561–571. Retrieved from http://www.sciencedirect.com/science/article/pii/S0022096513001331

Juliani, A. (2016). On tulpas - An analysis of imagined others. Retrieved from https://www.academia.edu/20174213/On_Tulpas_-_An_Analysis_of_Imagined_Others

Jean Piaget Society. Meeting (33rd : 2003 : Chicago, Ill.). (2007). Play and development: Evolutionary, sociocultural, and functional perspectives. Retrieved from Lawrence Erlbaüm website: http://www.psy.cmu.edu/~siegler/423-taylor07.pdf

Jeub, C. (2014, July 11). Thoughts on being an adult with imaginary friends. Retrieved from http://cynthiajeub.com/2014/07/thoughts-on-being-an-adult-with-imaginary-friends/

Kidd, E. (2012, June 21). *Imaginary friends: Evan Kidd at TEDxSydney* [Video file]. Retrieved from https://www.youtube.com/watch?v=UzCfUvWD0Q4

Lydon, D. (2011). Imaginary companions: Are they good for children? Retrieved from Trinity College Dublin website: http://psychology.tcd.ie/spj/past_issues/issue02/Reviews/%286%29%20David%20Lydon.pdf

McLeod, S. (2009). Attachment theory. Retrieved from http://www.simplypsychology.org/attachment.html

Randle, K. (2012, October 23). I have had an imaginary friend my entire life | Ask the Therapist. Retrieved from http://psychcentral.com/ask-the-therapist/2012/10/23/i-have-had-an-imaginary-friend-my-entire-life/

Roblyer, A. (2014, July 3). *Adults need more imaginary friends | Andrew Roblyer | TEDxTAMU* [Video file]. Retrieved from https://www.youtube.com/watch?v=JcKYIYwFf58

Root-Bernstein, M. (2008). Imaginary worldplay as an indicator of creative giftedness. Retrieved from L.V. Shavinina website: https://www.psychologytoday.com/files/attachments/1035/imaginary-worldplay-indicator-creative-giftedness.pdf

Sherman, J. E. (2013, November 11). Adults have imaginary friends too | Psychology Today. Retrieved from https://www.psychologytoday.com/blog/ambigamy/201311/adults-have-imaginary-friends-too

Stewart, E. (2016, March 14). PrimeMind | Tulpamancy: Imagining companions into existence. Retrieved from http://primemind.com/articles/hed-inside-the-uncanny-world-of-tulpamancy-a-community-that-s-imaging-companions-into-existence

Veissiere, S. (2015, April 3). Varieties of tulpa experiences: Sentient imaginary friends, embodied joint attention, and hypnotic sociality in a wired world | Somatosphere. Retrieved from http://somatosphere.net/2015/04/varieties-of-tulpa-experiences-sentient-imaginary-friends-embodied-joint-attention-and-hypnotic-sociality-in-a-wired-world.html

Printed in Great Britain
by Amazon